WREATHS

Techniques and Materials…Step-by-Step Projects… Creative Ideas for the Year Round

RICHARD KOLLATH

Photography by Robert Hoebermann

HOUGHTON MIFFLIN COMPANY · BOSTON

Copyright © 1988 by Michael Friedman Publishing Group, Inc.
All rights reserved

For information about permission to reproduce selections from
this book, write to Permissions, Houghton Mifflin Company,
2 Park Street, Boston, Massachusetts 02108.

Library of Congress Cataloging-in-Publication Data
Kollath, Richard.
Wreaths : techniques and materials, step-by-step projects,
creative ideas for the year round / Richard Kollath ;
photography by Robert Hoebermann.
p.   cm.
Reprint. Originally published: New York : Facts on File
Publications, 1988.
ISBN 0-395-55414-4
1. Wreaths.   I. Title.
[SB449.5.W74K64   1990]   90-32117
745.92 — dc20   CIP

Printed in the United States of America

LAP 10 9 8 7 6 5 4 3 2 1

Dedication

With great pride, I dedicate this book of wreaths to my parents, who provided me with perpetual gardens, love, and encouragement. And to the memory of my Grandfather Richard.

Acknowledgments

This book of wreaths has come about through the good will and talents of many friends and associates. It is with deep gratitude that I acknowledge their invaluable contributions.

To Michael Friedman and Karla Olson of the Friedman Group for seeing through an initial idea and supporting me during the critical early stages of development.

To Tim Frew, who patiently took my thoughts and edited them into a legible text.

To Mary Moriarty for continual support and trust in providing me the freedom with the rich variety of dried and preserved natural materials that added an essential dimension to the book.

To Barbara Miller of Hallmark Cards, Inc. for the candles and candlesticks that often accompany a wreath and for the many gift wrapping and party paper products used throughout the book.

To John Riccardi and Rudy Grant of Seagroatt Floral Supply Company for the beautiful air-dried miniature roses and the spectacular fresh roses that I dried in silica gel. Seagroatt roses are the absolute best.

To Nancy Jones of Bob's Candy Co. that so amply kept the holiday spirit alive in mid summer with their candy canes, peppermints, and delightful peppermint rings.

To Robert Palmatier and Fredric Misner, who so generously provided a number of antiques from their Stone Ridge, N.Y. shop, as well as permitted me to harvest grapevines from their property and to borrow their freshly canned jellies and tomatoes.

To Aleene for her thick designer tacky glue which I find a great necessity when working with dried and preserved flowers.

To Donald Goncalves for providing me with Thermogrip® brand hot melt glue guns and glue sticks from Emhart Home Products Division. The ease and efficiency using a hot melt glue gun for constructing so many of the wreaths was an essential tool and aid.

To Robert Hobermann whose sensitive eye and total understanding with the camera made the arduous task of photography a real pleasure. To Susan and Matthew for their patience and needed assistance.

To my wife Teri and son Jason who endured yet another inconvenience of having every available hook in our house occupied by a wreath. To them and everyone else, my sincerest appreciation and thanks.

C O N T E N T S

Introduction

Once exclusively a symbol of the Christmas season and its spirit, wreaths today are showing up in surprising places year-round. An herb wreath in the kitchen, a doily wreath in the bathroom or bedroom, a grapevine-and-dried-flower wreath as a permanent decoration in the living room, a quilted wreath in bright primary-color fabric in the family room—all of these appear more often as people explore the fun and beautiful possibilities of the never-ending circle. In addition, new wreathmakers are surprised to find that with a little imagination and a few basic techniques wreathmaking can be a deceptively simple way to create decorations and gifts.

In recent years, there has been a growing appreciation of traditional handicrafts as well as a renewed interest in gardening, cooking, decorating, and just about anything having to do with rural life. As a result, the art of wreathmaking has progressed far beyond the habitual evergreen wreath hanging on the door at Christmas. From simple country grapevine-and-herb wreaths to elaborate wreaths incorporating rare and exotic combinations of materials, this traditional rural handicraft has developed into an innovative and highly accessible art form.

Charming and imaginative wreaths can be constructed using everything from dried flowers to children's building blocks. While wreathmaking is only limited by the imagination, some materials and techniques do lend themselves to wreathmaking better than others. This book of beautiful wreaths is a treasure chest of ideas, techniques, and instruction. Some of the wreaths covered here you may want to copy vine-for-vine, flower-for-flower, while others you may wish to alter in ways that will best suit your particular taste or specific needs. Within each chapter I have provided the essential steps for constructing individual wreaths plus information on the kind of foundation used for each wreath. There are also helpful tips on executing specific designs as well as general information on topics such as preserving flowers, tying foundations, attaching unusual ornaments, and more.

It is fair to say that some of the wreaths illustrated here will be easier to duplicate than others. One reason is simply the availability of certain regional materials. However, one of the most enjoyable and challenging aspects of wreathmaking is the ability to make substitutions. You will find that any wreath will gradually take on characteristics that reflect your own creativity. Once you have completed one wreath, the door will remain open for continuing innovations and hours of enjoyment.

CHAPTER ONE
Getting Started

Wreathmaking can be a very rewarding experience, one that not only brings personal pride to the maker, but pleasure to all who see the results. Creating a wreath, like all productive efforts, requires the proper tools and adequate space. This is not to say that you can't make the most spectacular arrangement of materials in conditions less than perfect, but the better your work area the easier it may be for a more fluid and productive execution of your talents.

Basically, you need two surfaces to work with. I prefer a wall when making most of my wreath designs, but some wreaths can only be developed on a table top. In my studio I have a solid nail in a wall that is directly perpendicular to my table. I can simply pivot myself from one surface to the other with great ease and directness. I have sufficient room to step back and see how a wreath is developing on the wall, and yet be close enough to my worktable to have all the necessary tools and supplies at hand. I also have a large metal shelf unit at the far end of my worktable which houses boxes of supplies and dried materials.

A pegboard wall is a great place to store certain pieces of equipment and to hang wreaths that are in the process of completion. Obviously, the degree of complexity or sophistication of a work space can be quite varied. It is possible to clean off the kitchen table and work with an equally successful outcome.

What seems basic and most essential is that you have a good area to work in with few obstacles to interrupt the construction process. The work area should be well lit with both natural and electrical light sources. If you rely only on electrical lights, try to prevent shadows on the work surface. Experiment by adding or moving lights until the work area is as bright and evenly lit as possible. I use clip-on lights with aluminum light shields. They are flexible and inexpensive and are carried in all hardware stores.

If you are creating a specific space to work in and will keep that space for continued wreathmaking, then consider the height of your worktable. In my studio I use a piece of plywood placed on top of two sawhorses. What I like about the sawhorses is that I can remove the top clamps or brackets and break down the legs for easy storage.

It is very important to have an electrical outlet near your work area. You will often use a hot-glue gun in wreathmaking, and there is no greater frustration than having to hunt down an outlet or precariously stretch a lead from a faraway socket to your area. Good light, a proper and comfortable working height for your table, and a wall with a sturdy hook and an electrical outlet are the basics.

Complementing the basics is the proximity of adequate storage space. Gray industrial shelving is not only functional; it is also transportable. Easy to assemble and convenient to adjust, a wall of shelving can contain all the essentials you need from season to season. I gather and save all sorts of boxes, many in standardized proportions, that I fill and label and then stack on my shelves. Labelling them allows for stacking and not having to second-guess your memory as seasons pass. I purchase boxes if I have to, but also go to local merchants and see what they are discarding. Boxes with removable lids rather than fold-over tops are better, because they are easier to open and close.

Basic Tools

ONCE YOU HAVE CREATED A WORK SPACE, YOU WILL NEED the following tools to aid you in gathering materials and in constructing your wreaths.

A good pair of basic garden clippers, capable of cutting through fairly substantial twigs and small branches, and a fairly sharp folding pocketknife are essential for gathering materials. Both the clippers and knife should be able to fit comfortably in a pocket as you take to the woods or fields in your gathering pursuits. I often find that a small saw is also helpful to have along. Some saws are small enough to be fixed within a sheath and attached to a belt, yet capable of cutting through a small tree or large branch. I find a light bow saw with a blade protector an easy component to any expedition. Depending on where you're going and what you're gathering purposes are, scissors might also be a sensible tool to have.

For your work area you should have a pair of wire cutters, a pair of ribbon scissors, and a pair of garden shears to take care of your cutting needs. You will also quickly discover the value of a hot-glue gun as your wreathmaking interests expand. Hot-glue guns come in various sizes and price ranges. I have used a variety of them and prefer the larger ones with the trigger movement over the smaller ones, which operate by thumb pressure. What appeals to me is the freedom I have with the trigger gun, allowing better use of my hand and a greater ease in gluing. Both types work well, so research the various types to see which one best suits your wreathmaking needs.

A supply of craft wire (also called florist wire) is essential. This wire, available in both 22 and 24 gauge, is handy for attaching pods or flowers to wooden picks, making a secure loop for hanging, or tying bows and other elements to the wreath frame. You will also need wire to provide new stems for flowers that have been air-dried or silica-gel-dried.

While at the craft or florist shop, you will need to purchase wooden picks. These picks are either green or natural in color, and come in a variety of lengths—three inches, four inches, and six inches are the most common. They have a thin wire on top for attaching the flower to the pick. Buy several of each size and keep them in a labelled storage box with other materials.

Florist tape works well for disguising wires and securing materials. I like the dark-green or dark-brown colors, because they both blend with most of the materials I use. You'll find that with a little practice this tape is very easy to use. Simply start the end on a wire, then, with a gentle pull, spin the wire. The combination of pulling on the tape and spinning the wire will form a tight bond between the tape and the wire. A bottle or jar of white glue is also handy to have. I prefer the tacky designer glue, because it dries fastest and seems the most efficient to use. You will find through experimentation and through conversation with other wreathmakers what product or tool is best to perform certain techniques. Take note, and add that tool to your basic materials.

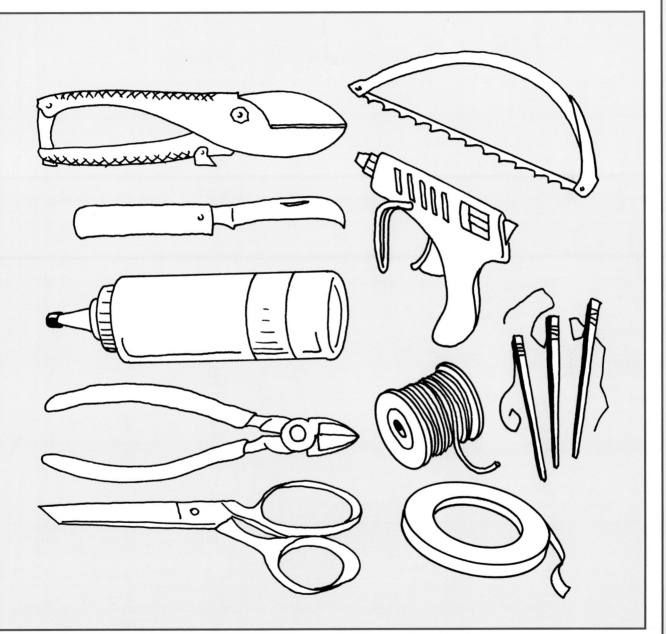

Kenneth Spengler

Basic Tools Needed for Drying

YOU MIGHT WANT TO BEGIN PRESERVING YOUR OWN flowers. To do so, you will need to choose between air-drying them or preserving them in silica gel. For air-drying flowers and pods you will need some rubber bands and kitchen twine, brown paper grocery bags, pushpins, cup hooks or nails, and either some screening or a drying rack.

To dry flowers with silica gel you will need boxes of silica gel, available through craft and florist shops, and storage boxes. I find plastic sweater boxes with tightfitting lids to work best. I also use masking tape to seal the lid of the box. Depending on which process you use, and on the durability of the flower, you will need additional boxes to store your preserved flowers. (See page 41 for more on preserving flowers with silica gel.)

Basic Wreath Forms

WE WILL DEVOTE INDIVIDUAL CHAPTERS TO THE CON-struction of wreath foundations as well as individual how-tos in making some of the illustrated wreaths within this book, but you should be familiar with the kinds of wreaths available to you through your local supply sources.

Grapevine wreaths come in sizes that range from three-inch (eight-centimeter) imported wreaths to very large, freshly wrapped wreaths. The industry, both floral and craft, has produced grapevine wreaths that not only come in natural colors but are also available in a palette of muted, vivid, or gilded colors. These colored wreaths spawn many decorative possibilities for your own creative expression. Wherever you find wreaths sold, you will also see heart shapes made of grapevine. They too come in natural as well as tinted colors.

Another popular wreath base that comes in a wide range of sizes is the straw wreath. Basically, this wreath is constructed of straw wound around a wire ring and secured with transparent nylon string. Straw wreaths come wrapped in a green plastic that is easy to remove. The straw wreath base is tight and full, where similar wreaths made of excelsior have a softer and denser feeling to them. Excelsior wreaths are available in both circular and heart shapes, just like straw-based forms, but come in a range of decorative colors. Predominantly a craft-store item, these wreaths seem to have gained popularity with craft classes.

Another versatile base is the Styrofoam base.

Two versions are readily available. One is the simple form cut from foam, either green or white, and having flat sides. The second type of foam wreath is extruded foam. This type is usually reinforced with a wire ring and is capable of holding heavier weight.

The last type of wreath base that is illustrated in this book is the wire ring. This, too, comes in a good range of sizes, as well as in heart shapes. They are versatile in making fresh garden wreaths and wonderful wreaths of permanent materials.

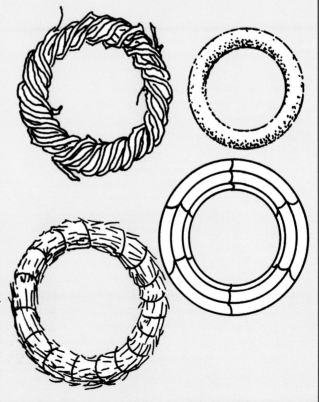

Kenneth Spengler

Things to Keep in Mind

IDEAS FOR WREATHS COME FROM MANY SOURCES. Scanning through magazines, browsing through store displays, visiting other areas of the country—wherever you look you are bound to find materials and concepts that will spark your interests. As you come across wreaths you would particularly like to copy, jot down a few notes on paper or try to sketch the general form. Ask about materials you do not recognize, and take advantage of walks through nature. Whether you're in the forest, at the seaside, or in your own backyard, you're sure to find something you can use for an attractive wreath. If you plant a garden, then you are in for an endless harvest of possibilities.

Remember that you will be working with a circle, one of the most basic shapes. There are constraints placed upon this elementary shape, in that it begins and ends in a continuous line and often has a consistent width. It is best to approach wreathmaking with the understanding that, while the circle usually provides the base on which to apply and fix materials, it is your own individual treatment of the various foundations and materials that will allow you the greatest freedom.

Experiment and improvise; some of the most beautiful wreaths have come from some of the most unusual combinations. You may choose to have long, trailing branches sweep the edge of your wreath and flow toward the floor, while clusters of pods and flowers burst unexpectedly from areas around the circumference.

When designing wreaths, scale is always an important consideration. Always keep in mind the intended resting place of the wreath as you are making it. If you want to hang it on your front door, it must fit your front door. There is very little that is more frustrating than spending hours constructing a wreath only to have it be too large or too small when it is finally finished. Avoid that frustration with careful planning and strategic execution. Your patience will reward you in the long run.

It is important to consider color when developing your wreath. In nature there is an incredible array of colors which can be combined to form wreaths of absolute poetry. Strong, bold colors, vivid to the senses, powerful to the eye, are but one experience when working with color. The subtle nuances that can come from combining delicate shades of one color family or variations of soft pastels are counterparts to the fully saturated tones of the bolder palette. There are no limits to the combinations of colors you can use, nor are there limitations to the scale of flowers or their textures.

Perhaps the most interesting wreaths are those that have an element of mystery and surprise to them. These unexpected qualities may easily come from a personalized interpretation of colors juxtaposed to one another, or to a surprising relationship in scale or texture. Visual richness, subtlety, and strength are all components to the overall texture of the wreathmaking process. To develop your skill in understanding more of this visual world, keep a watchful eye to the world as you walk in nature. Be aware of the unexpected and of the relationships of natural elements to each other. When you uncover a surprising quality about whatever it is you may be experiencing, translate that quality into your next wreath.

Nature, of course, is the obvious teacher, but you can also learn many things from the library. Check out books not only on floral construction but on painting and art in general. See how other creative people bring their art to life by relating textures and colors.

Another good idea is to keep a few of the elements you are working with at hand. Place a pod or a few dried flowers near where you work, away from the area where you are constructing your wreath, and occasionally look at the object, study it, and absorb it. Having a feeling for your materials will allow you the freedom to use unknown elements and still feel confident about your abilities. This confidence will let you experiment with colors that go beyond your personal preference, and soon you will be aware of your own growth as a creative person.

There are also some artistic elements to be aware of beyond color and texture. Scale *must* be considered. Choosing shapes and objects that work well within the proportions of your wreath will assure a visual balance. Establishing a rhythmic unity within the overall wreath is vital to its appearance. That is to say that your wreath should have a balance and counterbalance, each working to form a unified rhythmic whole. The flowing parts of the wreath should

blend and become comfortable to the eye.

One of the most rewarding experiences of all in the process of wreathmaking is the gathering process. Growing flowers, harvesting them, and drying them involves the planting, the nurturing, and finally the rewards from picking and drying. I air-dry some and silica-gel-dry some and am always pleased when I discover other materials on walks and planned harvesting excursions. What you need in terms of materials has been covered: sharp scissors or a good pair of clippers, possibly your pocketknife, and a good flat basket to carry your gathered flowers.

Here is a basic list of flowers and plants that work well in wreathmaking. This is for you to use as a reference, but by no means is this intended to limit your choices. Be willing to experiment with new materials all the time.

Wreathmaking Materials

ageratum, golden	carnation	delphinium	geranium	hyssop
ammobium	catmint	dock	gerbera	iris
anemone	celosia	eucalyptus	germander	jasmine
aster	chamomile	fennel	globe amaranth	jonquii
astilbe	coatmary	fern	goldenrod...in bud	joe-pye weed
baby's breath	cockscomb	feverfew	heliotrope	lady's-mantle
bellflower	cornflower	flax	hibiscus	lamb's ears
black-eyed Susan	daffodil	forget-me-not	hollyhock	larkspur
borage	dahlia	foxglove	honeysuckle	lavender
box calendula	daisy	freesia	hydrangea	lemon balm

Anita Marci

Anita Marci

Mary Close

20

Anita Marci

Mary Close

Mary Close

lemon leaves	Queen Anne's lace	rue	teasel
lilac	pansy	sage	thistle
lily	pearly everlasting	salvia	thyme
lily-of-the-valley	peony	sea holly	tulip
loosestrife	petunia	silver king	Veronica
marigold	pink	southernwood	violet
monkshood	pussy willow	statice	wild grass
mint	ranunculus	stock	wormwood
mugwort	rose	strawflower	yarrow
nasturtium	rose leaf	sunflower	zinnia
orange blossom	rosemary	tansy	

CHAPTER TWO

Grapevine Wreaths

To me, there is nothing more satisfying than to travel the countryside in search of grapevines. With garden clippers and a thermos of hot coffee in hand, the hunt becomes one of fall's greatest adventures. It is best to harvest grapevines in the autumn, when they are brown and the leaves are turning golden. Early-summer vines are too green and will crack at the simplest bend, causing unnecessary frustration.

If you choose not to weave your own grapevine wreaths, you can buy them at most flower, garden, and craft shops. Popular as well as plentiful, they are available in a number of sizes and surface treatments—including the ever-popular vine heart, a number of which are illustrated throughout this book.

On a loosely woven, handmade vine wreath, I have randomly applied preserved autumn leaves around the wreath form with a hot-glue gun. The colors of the leaves vary from rust to a bright yellow. I have intertwined them with the wreath in such a way that they stick out prominently in some places but are tucked within the ribs of the vines in others. This gives the wreath its natural, spontaneous look. Three sea-grape leaves form a focal point at the top of the composition. Garden strawflowers provide color and scale contrast to the natural pinecones that cluster around the wreath. Lovely lavender statice travels throughout the warmer strawflower's colors, tying all the neutral elements together, while the lunaria, or silver dollars, add luster to the overall composition with patches of lightness.

This harvest wreath uses materials that are easily available through local garden shops, craft stores, and florists; growing your own strawflowers, statice, and silver dollars makes for an even more satisfying wreath at harvest time. Adding materials such as sea-grape leaves brings an unexpected element of surprise to the wreath.

How to Make a Grapevine Base

THE PROCESS OF MAKING A GRAPEVINE WREATH IS RE-ally a very simple one that becomes even more so with practice. Hold the cut end of a vine in your left hand, and with your right hand bend the free end of the vine into a circle, approximating the desired proportion of the final wreath. Clasp that section of the vine with your left hand. Your hand now holds the loop that will become the wreath. With your right hand weave the free end of the vine in and out, through the loop, securing the two ends by locking them into the vine.

Start your second length of vine by inserting one end into the woven part of the first loop. Weave the length of the second vine through the wreath and secure the ends. With each length of vine your wreath will grow in width. Continue this process until you achieve the desired fullness. When ending the wreath, tuck all the loose ends into the body of the wreath.

Another method of making a vine wreath is to start with three vines, and, while holding them in your left hand, twist them together so that they form a rope-like singular vine. When adding additional vines, continue to twist each one around the wreath so that the final, full wreath is even and dense. Again, tuck all loose ends into the body of the wreath after you've reached the desired width.

I always prefer to make my wreaths very full and somewhat irregular instead of even and pristine. The reasoning is that the wreath will be able to hold more objects in unexpected places if it is strong and full—allowing more freedom in the design.

After wrapping my wreaths I always add a wire loop to the top for hanging. This gives me a reference point for the top of the wreath as well as a safeguard for holding the vines together. Be sure the wire loop is strong and securely attached. Many hours of fine work can be lost in an instant if your creation falls off the hook because of a loose wire. If you finish your wreath and realize you forgot to add a hanging wire, be very careful not to harm your work when threading the wire through the vine. An extra pair of hands can be very welcome.

Although wrapping a grapevine wreath is relatively easy, it is very important to pay attention to how tight you wrap the vines as you go along. The degree of firmness or looseness of the vine will strongly influence the final look of the wreath. Experimentation is the key here. The more wreaths you make, the greater control you will have. No matter what size wreath you are attempting, the process is the same; always remember to lock the starting vines together and weave in the remaining vines. If you finish a vine base that satisfies your needs, but still have extra vines, take the time to wind another, perhaps smaller wreath. The excitement of making a wreath is such that when you have completed one you'll most likely want to begin another. Remember, too, that a small wreath is always a great gift to have on hand; so make extras to "save for a rainy day."

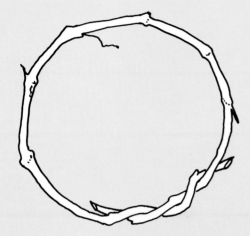 

In method one, wrap one length of vine at a time, weaving new lengths around the main body of the wreath until reaching the desired width.

In method two, start with three vines and twist them together so they form a ropelike singular vine. Add more vines to reach the desired width.

Kenneth Spengler

While exploring the forest floor or open fields in the fall, or while taking a holiday to another part of the country, you are bound to come across some unusual pods or other dried materials. Such discoveries can be exciting and can lead to wonderful collections. While these natural treasures make some of the most rewarding wreath materials, many very exotic flowers, pods, and plants are available through your local florist and craft stores and can add much to your overall wreath design. These materials are collected from all over the world and made ready for your creative use.

In this example, I have wrapped some lengths of bleached vines around a natural vine wreath and have then added clusters of sea-grape leaves as well as an array of bleached and preserved pods. Chico, chokeberry, curly protea, flat canella, and sponge mushrooms all add their independent shapes and textures in bringing a harmonic blend of browns and beiges to this wreath. If you can't find the specific pod you want, substitute nuts, pinecones, bits of bark, or even cork to carry on the monochrome palette of this design.

*I*n order to achieve the delicate lacy feeling of this wreath, I covered a pre-made vine heart base with sprigs of fresh silver king. Pieces of thin florist's wire works well for attaching the fragile silver king into place. The preserved yellow flowers add a warm contrast to the soft gray of the silver king. The addition of fresh bayberry and bud clusters from flat-leaf eucalyptus complement the overall gray coloration, while keeping their own independence. To bring out the pale green of the eucalyptus, I added a soft moss-green ribbon with a subtle edge of gold. Lavender statice provides a color complement to the yellow flowers. I used a hot-glue gun to attach all the components together. Again, always remember to first attach a hanging hook to your frame before adding any elements to the wreath.

*M*any wreaths are meant to last—to echo the season and reflect the beauty of nature for as long as the materials hold up. Some wreaths, however, are spontaneous expressions of a particular moment in time.

In this fall celebration, baby pumpkins, gourds, bittersweet, strawflowers, and sunflowers unite with the bold vibrancy of cockscombs, Japanese lanterns, and vivid purple statice; the expression becomes a magnificent salute to the brilliant energies of fall. This composition was placed upon a richly dyed burgundy grapevine wreath in order to help bring out the intense colors and bold shifts in scale of each element. Many pre-made vine wreaths come in a spectacular array of colors—boldly saturated as well as pastel. Vine colors can be used to enhance or complement the added materials—as in this example. When you make a wreath such as this, understand that it may go through some natural changes, so be ready to continue adding other durable elements as some of the more perishable ones depart. A wreath can become an ongoing adventure.

Here, the bittersweet seems to explode from the regimented contour of the wreath form, much as it does when growing in the wild. Other elements, such as the gourds and the Japanese lanterns, are clustered in groups. The whole composition nearly fills the substructure, but leaves just enough visible base to enjoy the unexpected colored vine. Although this wreath is hung, consider laying it flat as a centerpiece on a holiday table.

The personality of the vine wreath itself is sometimes the element that first speaks to the viewer. There are a number of choices when making them. In this wreath I used rather thick vines to determine the finished form. I intentionally left great holes within the structure of the wreath while enhancing the natural beauty of the grape-vine with the inclusion of fresh clusters of grapes and grape leaves. As the grapes and the leaves dried they became very brittle but still retained their leafy identity. While sometimes I feel that a smooth, uniform wreath is more suitable for a specific design, here I pre-ferred to allow much of the nature of the grapevine to come forth. The deep and open segments in the vine construction are natural places to cluster cockscomb, yarrow, and stems of flat-leaf eucalyptus. Small branches of fresh bayberry bring a lighter tonal value to the deeper, more intense colors of the yarrow and cocks-comb. The contrast helps the eye to travel around the composition.

How to Air-dry Flowers

MOST OF THE FLOWERS USED IN THE PREVIOUS WREATH are air-dried—a simple process anyone can do without much trouble. To air-dry flowers from your garden, simply pick the individual flowers during the drier part of the day, when the dew has evaporated and the sun has begun to warm the earth. Strip their leaves and tie them into small bunches of three to five stems. Hang the stems up in a dry, dimly lit part of the house, such as an attic or a closet. Try to avoid dusty places. If that isn't possible, then place your flowers in a large paper bag, tying the top of the bag to the flower stems. Invert the bag and hang to dry. Drying time will depend on the amount

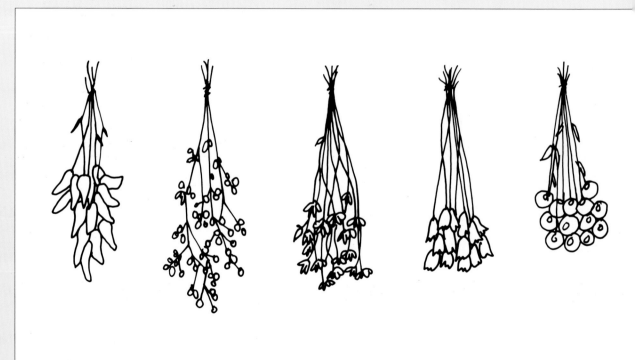

of air, heat, and moisture in the room. Check the flowers from day to day and remove them when the flower petals feel like paper and are no longer soft and pliable. When storing the dried flowers, keep them away from excessive moisture and direct sunlight. Both conditions will shorten the life of the flower.

Kenneth Spengler

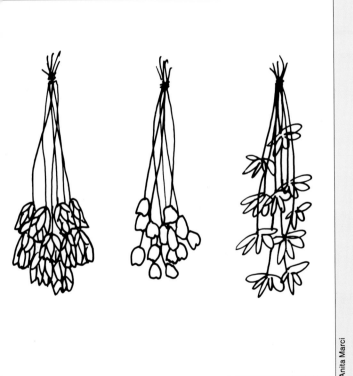

Anita Marci

Another method for air-drying flowers is to lay them on a screen in the attic or under a guest-room bed. Newspaper also works, as long as you remember the necessary ingredients— low light and warm, dry air. Experimentation is essential in determining what works best for your particular situation.

This hydrangea wreath is another example of a wreath that celebrates a specific moment in the evolution of fall. It consists of only hydrangeas, a flower made up of many smaller flowers. Although they have different tonalities and sizes, their appearance expresses a general unity. There is a soft fullness to the flower, and delicate shadings of color. Using a variety of blossom sizes and weaving them into a very aggressive vine wreath brings two juxtaposed elements into a unified whole. Allowing the vine to dominate the positioning of the flowers, I hot-glued the hydrangeas throughout the large-scaled wreath. The uniformity of the flowers and subtle blending of the coloration keeps the scale of the wreath under control.

This pre-made heart with silica-gel dried wild roses is akin to the hydrangea wreath in that both use a single flower and expose some of the vine structure. While the great swells of the hydrangea bring that wreath its softness, the rose heart relies on the relationship of the sparse, delicate rose to the heart shape. Rose clusters are placed along the sides of the heart, while vertically placed roses join together in the junction at the top. The leaves enhance the heart shape, fill in the width, and support the sprigs of rose clusters. I took special care to match the scale of the heart to the scale of the flowers—as I did for the hydrangea wreath above. Scale is an important factor in establishing a visual presence to the wreath. If the elements are too large, it may become overpowering; if they're too small or sparse, it may lack interest. Balance, scale, rhythm, and color relationships are major considerations when making a wreath. (See Chapter One, "Getting Started," for more discussion of these topics.)

This strawflower wreath is another example of the use of a pre-made vine heart. Here, I harvested my own strawflowers and then inserted florist wire into the heads of each flower and hung them to dry.

When they were ready, I first attached the lighter strawflowers with a hot-glue gun around the heart in a way that evenly distributed the color variations. Next I brought in a darker flower tone, and after that the deepest colors. Finally, I included the white sprigs of stringia, which added a lightness in scale and color to the overall warm, dense composition.

Fill an airtight container about two-thirds full with silica gel, gently place the flowers on top, and then gently sprinkle more gel on top until the flowers are completely covered. Seal the container for about three or four days. When the flowers are completely dry, carefully remove them with a slotted spoon.

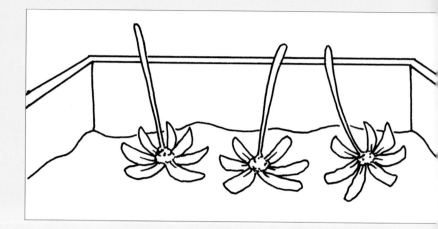

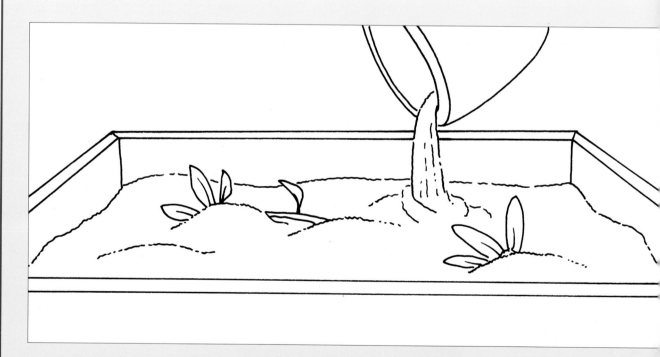

Drying Flowers with Silica Gel

IT IS A GREAT FEELING TO GO INTO YOUR GARDEN AND PICK flowers or herbs that you've grown, bring them back to your house, and use them, either directly in cooking, in a fresh arrangement, or drying them for use at a later time. It is also sad when seasons change and you no longer have the special flowers of spring or early summer to use or appreciate. Silica gel allows you the privilege of saving what is usually transitory.

Silica gel is a sand-like substance that dries flowers within a few days. It can be purchased at most flower or craft stores and is very convenient to use. All you need is a box of gel and a few airtight container such as plastic storage boxes. The process of drying must be done in airtight containers to prevent outside moisture from reaching the flowers. The silica gel removes moisture from the flowers, making them usable for wreaths as well as dried arrangements and potpourri.

Here are a few basic steps in drying flowers with silica gel. Fill an airtight containers about two-thirds full with the gel. Lay each flower in the gel, petals up. Very gently sprinkle the remaining gel around and over each flower, being careful to fill in between the petals, until the flowers are completely covered. Seal the container and in three days check the progress. In most cases I have found that three or four days does the trick, but heavy-stemmed, thick-petaled flowers may require more time.

Removing the dried flowers is perhaps the trickiest part of the process, because they have now become very fragile and can easily break apart. The best method is to place a slotted spoon under the petals and gently lift the flower out. After removing the flowers, store them in another plastic box with a quarter inch (four millimeters) of gel covering the bottom.

This process allows you to keep out-of-season flowers for use later on, providing a floral vocabulary that extends the range and variety of flowers year-round. The silica-gel process works not only with homegrown flowers but with store-bought flowers as well. The key element to remember is that the flowers should be dry and fresh when placed in the gel. The fresher the flower, the more successful the result. This is also a trial-and-error process, so don't become discouraged if the petals fall off your first batch. Glue works wonders and can be used to replace a missing petal.

Kenneth Spengler

Use a paint brush and a small bit of glue to replace any petals that may have fallen off.

This small, handmade vine wreath is ornamented with silica-gel-dried black-eyed Susans, a few acorns, and preserved leaves. Many of the twigs from the original grapevine are still attached. The inherent rhythm of this wreath comes from the juxtaposition of the twigs around the wreath form and the variation in scale of the dried flowers. It is made up of individual clusters of flowers, with equal space allotted for the vine itself. With this wreath it is important to show as much of the wreath form as possible in order to take advantage of the unique, personal quality of the attached twigs.

*T*raditionally, wreaths have been used as decorative accents at times of celebration. The festive presence of this wedding wreath almost seems to ring in an abundant sound of joy through the many paper bells attached to the pre-made, white-painted vine wreath. Silver ribbon and silver stars accent the fullness of the wedding bells, and add to the festiveness of the wreath. It should be mentioned that all wreaths need not be made of flowers and that a wreath of wrapped packages makes a wonderful holiday or birthday centerpiece, each child or adult receiving a gift as the packages are taken from the wreath. Holiday bells in red and green are a perfect accompaniment to evergreens or a painted vine base. The fact is that there are many unusual materials that can make delightful and unique wreaths. Visit card stores, craft shops, and floral shops, and keep abreast of new ideas.

A variation on this wreath is to add fresh flowers by inserting them into water picks, available at your local florist, and placing them amidst the bells. Your wreath can become as complex as you wish, as long as you keep the design proportionate to the base. This wedding-bell wreath can be taken apart, as the bells collapse and are simply tied onto the wreath. This allows you the opportunity to create another festive wedding wreath when the next bride calls.

This wreath offers some unusual yet simple ideas for a colorful party decoration. Spray-paint a vine wreath a solid color, then hand-paint some stripes that correspond to gift wrapping paper or party favors and add yards of curling ribbon. Wrap packages for each child in the colors of the wreath, then take the whole party out into the fields, your backyard, or someplace where fun has no boundaries. The scale and colors of this party wreath can be altered to fit a number of situations and environments.

resh flowers attached to a wreath do very well for a limited period of time if they are first placed in water tubes. As mentioned before, water tubes are available through your florist in a number of shapes and sizes. Add a few fresh flowers, perhaps a bright ribbon, and hang this beautiful and seasonal presentation on your door. It will reflect your creativity as well as the completeness of your party preparations.

A variation on this wreath would be to add some small succulents or some ivy. In all the examples within this book there are many variations and substitutions that can be made. If you don't have a particular ingredient for one of these wreaths, improvise. You will be surprised at how varied a wreath can be.

*S*pring flowers, again in water tubes; an abandoned bird's nest; a few feathers picked up on vacation, some tropical, others domestic—each of these elements were added for their particular form and color. When the pussy willows appear and winter still has a leg in the door, cheer up your house or table with a spring wreath. It may only last a few days, but it will bridge the changing of the seasons. Create a fresh-flower wreath for a special party or meeting, or as a "thinking-of-you" gift. By refilling the water picks you can lengthen the life of the fresh flowers and thus prolong the beauty of the wreath. You may want to design the wreath so that when you remove the flowers, and their water tubes, you have the bird's nest and a few colorful feathers left to enjoy. If you are making this wreath for Easter, try blowing out some eggs, dyeing or painting them bright colors, and hot-gluing them among the flowers, thus making this wreath both fuller and more festive.

47

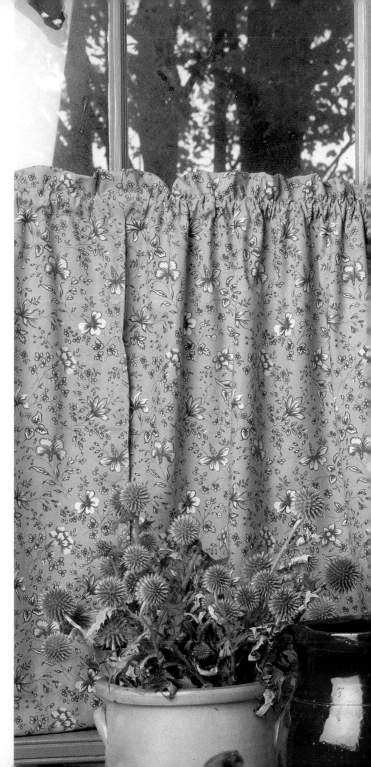

$\mathcal{A}$lthough this particular heart is pre-made, it is a simple process to make your own. First make a beginning, heart-shaped form out of wire—a coat hanger will do. Then place the cut grapevines onto the heart shape and, with thin florist wire, wire them in place. It is possible to attach three or four vines at once to create a fuller form. Always remember to use a thin-gauge florist wire to secure the vines. You will want to cover the construction with flowers when finished. Also remember to always place a hanging hook at the top of every wreath before adding any ornaments. A finished wreath can be very cumbersome to handle.

This heart has a combination of commercially dried black-eyed Susans, as well as a few pansies, some lichen, and pieces of sheet moss. A few sprigs of bayberries and a satin ribbon add to the ingredients. The combined use of silica-gel flowers and available dried flowers provides a personalized touch to the wreath. The use of the unexpected adds great charm and alters the finished look of your creation.

A commercially bleached wreath with pods, yellow roses, and cornhusks makes this tailored wreath appear very snug. Clusters of cornhusk loops form a generous bow at the top of the wreath. This cluster mirrors a similar cluster of yellow roses and pods. The cornhusk loops were wired onto short florist picks and directly inserted into the wreath structure. A touch of glue from a hot-glue gun holds each pick in place. The dried roses, ferns, and pods were also glued fast to prevent them from falling off. A tailored wreath of such paleness and symmetry can be used in a number of settings throughout the home for a variety of occasions.

*W*hereas the previous wreath feels hard and very controlled, this sumptuous heart evokes a purely romantic feeling. It employs a great variety of summer flowers, mixing together colors and textures as well as scales. Using silica-gel dried flowers hot-glued onto a pre-made heart base, this heart includes the richest examples of the early-summer garden and the late-spring bounty. Peonies, summer roses, wild sunflowers, Queen Anne's lace, and black-eyed Susans from the fields combine with sprigs of wild roses and bachelor's buttons. Shades of orange and pink, deep rich reds, and vibrant blues nest together with a few wild leaves. The heart has symmetry and fullness while evoking lovely surface grace and beauty.

*I*n early fall I often make a large vine wreath and begin collecting fallen bird's nests, a wasp's nest or two, and dried sunflowers. I gather them together to make an ongoing fall-through-winter wreath. They become gatherings, each version an addition or subtraction to the last, and always dependent on the wonders that are found in nature. A branch or two of brilliant-colored leaves enhances the kaleidoscope of colors that grace the gathering wreath. When the snows cover the land, I like to add berries of cedar and juniper to the vine, along with winter redberries and evergreen boughs. If pineapples or apples weather the fall, they can be used as a simple base for found objects. I like to keep the bold bare wreath for the rest of the year and hang it on the outside of a building—both to fill the space and to re-call the wreath's earlier wardrobes.

CHAPTER THREE

Wire Wreaths

*T*here are endless possibilities for creating beautiful and imaginative wreaths—the chapter on grapevines only tapped the surface. The basic truth about wreathmaking as a handicraft is that the possibilities are endless. Your explorations can be as varied as flowers are available. By changing one flower or a combination of flowers in one wreath design, you can come up with what looks like an entirely different wreath.

Wire rings are a very useful base on which to construct a wreath. They are available in a number of sizes and weights to support various sizes and weights of ornaments. Be careful when selecting the ring: Make sure that it will suit your requirements. As in preparing to make a wire wreath —and with *all* wreaths—remember to attach a hanging loop.

For this lovely heart wreath I wired sprigs of fresh rosemary, sage, and mint to the base and then used a hot-glue gun to attach strips of cinnamon to the herbs. At the top of the heart, delicate silica-gel-dried roses were glued into place along with a few small pinecones. The deep brown of the pinecones complements the soft golden color of the rose. This wreath is secure, because the wire holding the fresh herbs has a firm grip on the wire base and the hot-glue does a tremendous job of anchoring the light elements.

𝒜nother small wreath constructed from a wire base is this moss-covered wreath with pink roses and dusty miller. Apply hot glue to the sheet moss and carefully fold it around and over the wire frame, squeezing it to form a snug covering. Add more moss if necessary, until you achieve the desired fullness. When the moss is secure, attach clusters of rose hips, individual leaves from a dusty miller plant, and some beautifully opened silica-gel-dried roses with a hot-glue gun. Rose hips can be found in the wild during autumn, or they can be bought from your florist along with the roses. Allow the roses to open before you dry them, but keep in mind that for best results it is important to dry flowers when they are fresh. Pop the roses into the gel as soon as they reach the degree of openness you desire.

To dry dusty miller, either dry individual leaves on a screen or pop them into the silica gel, too. I find air-drying whole plants to be interesting.

ire rings are wonderful to use after harvesting a group of flowers and herbs from the garden. The entire picking process is heightened by the expectation of turning the fruits of your garden into a beautiful dried wreath that will last for a year or more. A great deal of satisfaction can be gained from growing, harvesting, and drying virtually all of your wreath materials. This wreath is entirely made up of materials grown in my garden.

62

Winding a Wreath

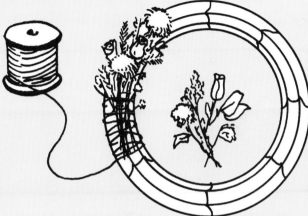

Kenneth Spengler

TO WIND A WREATH ON A WIRE FRAME YOU FIRST NEED TO clear off a good working surface (see Chapter One—Getting Started). A kitchen table is fine, as is a workbench or picnic table. If your knees are good and your back isn't stiff, the ground works equally well. You will need a pair of garden snippers, a spool of waxed twine made for winding wreaths (waxed twine grips the flower stems better than unwaxed), and, of course, a wire ring with a loop at the top.

Begin to make a general selection of what flowers you have and what additional material you expect to put into your wreath. The only hitch in winding a wreath is that once you begin it is not possible to stop and add additional elements, so be sure to plan ahead.

After deciding what elements you will be using, take a few of the flowers and place them on the wire frame. Hold the frame and the flowers in your left hand and place a length of twine alongside the flower stems. With your right hand, wind the spool of twine through and around the wreath in a clockwise direction and secure the twine so that it doesn't unravel. Be sure to wind a few turns around the wreath with each cluster of flowers, making sure all elements are tight and secure. This process of winding in a clockwise direction in a continual spiral motion is the manner in which the entire wreath will be wound. Each time you have secured a handful of flowers to the frame, reapply another cluster of flowers or herbs. An important note: include small bunches of flowers so that they cover the outer and inner edges of the wreath.

When you are nearly at the end of the wreath and are approaching the starting point, be extra careful that you don't bruise the lead flowers. Gently lift their heads up and place the stems of the tail-end flowers into place, wind with care, and finally secure the twine with a few good knots. If the construction has a noticeable gap, I sometimes take a few flowers, wire them to a short florist pick, and insert the pick into the open area.

Don't worry about using too many flowers in a winding wreath; a fuller wreath seems to look better than one where the mechanics are exposed. This winding process allows you to make a number of wreath combinations using a great variety of materials, as well as a number of ring sizes. The more practice you have, the easier this process will become.

*T*he following two examples are really variations on the autumn combinations seen in the previous wreath. Each wreath has used a selection of strawflowers, sage, rosemary, German statice (which is white), colored statice, silver king, yarrow, nigella, dried roses, and a pod or two.

Variations on the fullness and overall texture are up to you. To make multiple wreaths of a particular style, simply note the general amount of materials needed and reserve an equal portion for the next wreath.

*J*ust like the grapevine wreaths, wire frames are available in both rings and heart forms. This Southwest chili heart was made by opening one end of the heart frame and stringing on enough chilis to form a compact line of peppers. The ends at the lower point of the heart frame are joined together by two loops. This makes a great wreath that comple-ments the decor of any kitchen, and is a wonderful gift for someone who is fond of cooking.

*P*aper ribbon is a popular item available at craft stores and florist shops. Here, I covered a small wire ring with paper ribbon, culminating with a big paper bow on the top. Next, I strung small red peppers on a sturdy thread and wound them around the covered frame, securing both ends behind the bow. I then wired garlic and a few sprigs of sage onto the knot of the bow. This little wreath is right at home in the kitchen, where the cook can systematically remove the ingredients throughout the winter and then refill the wreath come late summer.

*T*his harvest wreath of strawberry popcorn and silver king was made by using waxed twine and a medium-sized wire frame. To wind this wreath, I began with the center ear, adding a few pieces of silver king and ears to cover the inner and outer edges of the wreath. Because the popcorn ears are heavy, it is very important to wind a few extra turns of the twine so that the wreath remains very tight. The silver king softens the overall dominance of the cornhusks, and breaks up the beige that would otherwise overpower the wreath.

The last illustration of a wire wreath is this full rose-hip wreath, which uses the same winding construction as the previous few wreaths. Simply gather the rose-hip clusters in small bunches and wind the twine to secure. A real warning: Rose hips are very difficult to harvest; their sharp thorns can prick your arms and hands.

70

CHAPTER FOUR

Straw-based Wreaths

The straw base is perhaps the most versatile of all wreath bases. It consists of tightly packed rings of straw bound together by a transparent thread. Coming in a number of sizes, the girth of straw wreaths makes them especially suitable for inserting picked material. You can purchase straw wreaths in nearly all florist shops, craft stores, and even some fabric centers.

This wreath of wheat, rye, and wild oats was made by taking three or four pieces of each element, one by one, and wiring them onto a three-inch (8 = centimeter) wooden pick. I then followed a clockwise direction, inserting each element into the straw until the whole wreath was covered by a gentle blending of the three different materials. This blending creates a change in the texture of the wreath and an interplay with light that shifts the tonalities of the overall complexion of the wreath. The result is a monochrome wreath that is still very complex in its texture and surface. Try different variations of this wreath by substituting different grasses from the fields or by using only one material and varying its length and texture.

75

For this harvest wreath I twisted long lengths of raffia together and wrapped them onto the lower portion of a straw ring. I then added corn and chili peppers to the top of the wreath to complete the Southwest flavor. The small ears of corn were attached by wiring them onto florist picks and inserting them into the wreath. The corn became a cascade, as one ear overlapped another, forming a great tuft of husks at the top. The small hot peppers were strung on a durable string and tied around the central stack of husks. By allowing the raffia to remain a little free, I feel I created a more interesting texture.

This autumn-leaf wreath is yet another example of using florist's picks to attach wreath materials to the base. Using oak leaves that were treated to remain flexible, I chose colors that flowed from yellow to orange to rust and attached them in a process very similar to the wheat construction (page 75). Broad color areas direct the eye around the wreath and aid in creating the sweeping movement of color within the wreath.

*I*t seemed essential to include a straw heart, as we have used heart frames within each chapter. Here I have combined the straw heart with one of the most traditional wreath forms—the pinecone wreath. There are many ways to make a pinecone wreath, the most common one being to wire each pinecone and to individually attach them according to size around a double wire frame. Many wonderful patterns develop from the varying sizes and textures of pinecones.

This pinecone heart is a departure from the very exacting methods of wire-frame construction. A straw-heart base is the support for pre-picked pinecone rosettes—available through your source centers. The picks are already inserted into the crown of the cone, making the process of creating the symmetrical heart relatively simple. First, sort out the rosettes according to size. Starting with the smaller cones, begin attaching the rosettes in such a way that they form patterns of textural interest.

80

*T*his moss-and-lichen wreath is another very simple wreath to construct. Using sheet moss to cover the straw base, I added pieces of wood moss, reindeer moss, and giant reindeer moss, each available through florist shops, as well as lichen that I picked up on a walk through the woods. The fullness of this wreath is an exercise in placement. The hot-glue gun easily set down the general distribution of the colors and variety of textures provided by the moss. The challenge is to create interesting clusters for the eye so that the general texture of the wreath is not monotonous. The characteristics of each moss made it possible to attach each clump to another at angles that enhance the overall rhythm of the wreath surface. Bits of leaves and pine needles have been left in the lichen to extend the natural charm of this wreath.

*H*ere, I covered a very small heart of straw with a coat of sheet moss, glued down with a hot-glue gun. A cluster of pansies and Johnny-jump-ups, all dried in silica gel, ornaments the surface. The size variations and color changes keep the surface of this heart interesting. It is a perfect little wreath for a gift—delicate and special through the combinations of moss and flowers, as well as its general scale.

his summer wreath consists of preserved ferns covering a straw wreath. The vivid green fern brings out the deep magenta of the cockscomb, the pale contrast of the bleached grapevine, the burgundy to gold shading of the strawflowers, and the soft lavender statice. There are a number of treated ferns available through your florist. Each will bring a grace and softness to a wreath while adding the summer spirit to other flowers.

In this example, small clusters of the fern were wired to florist's picks and inserted into the straw base. When the wreath was full, I took longer lengths of the fern and picked them among the shorter clusters, which extended the flowing softness of the surface. It is important to allow the edge of the wreath a little freedom of movement. Once the fern was placed, I wired the ends of the bleached grapevine onto picks, anchored one end to the base, and weaved the vine through the center of the wreath into a pleasing rhythm before securing the other end to the wreath frame. Finally, I added a few sprigs of baby's breath to lighten the whole wreath and add a lovely summer touch. Each flower was either picked or placed with the help of the hot-glue gun.

The broadness of the straw base allows for real expansion when winding a wreath (see page 63 for information on winding a wreath). This example has been made by winding using waxed twine, though some elements have been picked into the finished wreath. This is truly a fall symphony of all flowers, both air-dried as well as purchased, including fresh herbs and lengths of cinnamon. To duplicate this wreath, you could combine garden flowers, store-bought flowers, and any unexpected wild things you might find. One of the greatest delights in wreathmaking is that you can use virtually any material as long as you are pleased with the general tonalities of the entire composition.

There is a great deal of activity going on with this silica-gel-dried wreath. Flowers peek out from underneath others; colors brush against colors; petals intermingle with leaves. Pink peonies, pale-yellow tiger lilies, bright-hued zinnias, and delicate delphinium contrast against the more vivid deep orange and yellow of summer daisies, black-eyed Susans, and bachelor buttons. Among the varieties of flowers I used are wild roses and marigolds; bits of pale lichen and deeper-colored sheet moss assist in filling in some of the visual pockets. Each flower was dried in silica gel, a process that took many weeks and may easily be the final statement of a season's labor. The wreath is tightly constructed, yet the random leaves fall into an irregular pattern, allowing the eye to move about in a less regimented way. Keep an unexpected spirit to your wreaths and they will remain interesting to you and to others for a long period of time.

This picked pod wreath creates a bold impression with its tones of whitewashed gray. There is a boldness and directness to each element, and from the beginning to the end each pod holds its own space with its own distinctive shape. Although these whitewashed pods are available from your local florist, it is also possible to do the job yourself. All you need are a few old rags, a bucket of white paint, and a two-inch (five-centimeter) brush to penetrate all the deep crevices in the pods. I suggest using water-soluble acrylic paint to keep the cleaning-up process as simple as possible.

Simply dip each pod into the bucket of paint until the paint saturates the pod. Remove the pod from the bucket and let the excess drip off. Then gently wipe off more paint until there is a thin, even coat of paint on the pod.

When you place the pods into the straw base, fill in the wreath with individual pods, then add some sprigs of German statice to soften the overall line of the wreath. The statice is similar in color to the pods, but has a softness that provides a textural contrast to the more rigid pods, lending a balance to the overall wreath.

One of the great joys of wreathmaking is that it can be done just for the fun of it. A remembrance of a summer vacation by the sea can become the foundation for a beautiful summer wreath. Here, Spanish moss was hot-glued to the straw frame to form the base for the decorative shells. I attached the shells to florist picks with a hot-glue gun and then inserted them into the wreath at angles, in order to keep the surface alive with an independent energy. Black-eyed Susans and lovely blue larkspur flowers were glued among the shells and pieces of coral. The finishing touch to this wreath came with a thin satin bow with trailing streamers. The ribbon added an element of grace to the wreath.

Remember to alter the scale of the shells you use so that the wreath doesn't feel too regulated, and keep the shells at soft angles to one another. This, too, keeps the surface more alive. What appears in nature is an ever-changing cycle, an ever-moving line. A wreath should seem almost alive as it hangs on your wall or graces your table.

A very similar foundation to straw is Styrofoam, in that it comes in about the same sizes and dimensions. There are some advantages to working with Styrofoam, one being that the stems of flowers penetrate it rather easily. It is lightweight and holds most materials very well. My principle objection to Styrofoam is that it has a tendency to split when you use heavy materials so it must be reinforced. However, I do find it a very suitable base for the wreaths illustrated here.

This harvest wreath was constructed using a repetitive spiral placement, employing a variety of materials, each represented by an individual color and texture. Pink larkspur, gray silver king, deep cranberry, and pale-green sage are the dominating arms of this wheel, while nigella, yarrow, and purple statice add their complementary textures.

Each stem was inserted directly into the Styrofoam. It is important to make sure to cover the inside and outside edges of the wreath and to cut the stems according to your specific needs.

The same construction techniques were used in making this eucalyptus wreath: Short lengths of the stems were cut and directly inserted into the foam base. Longer lengths were then added to give the wreath fullness as well as grace. Once again, the stem lengths were cut at varying lengths to avoid the possibility that the final wreath would look as if a computer made it. Life for a wreath comes through the play of one element against another.

I enjoy making wreaths using basically only one type of material. Again, this silver-king wreath was constructed the same way as the eucalyptus wreath on the previous page.

My only words of advice in making a wreath of this type are to keep it free, open, and loose. Let the sunlight play off the surface and watch the beautiful inner shadows develop throughout the day and in the changing season. This wreath, like the eucalyptus wreath, can be hung almost anywhere and makes a perfect gift.

To construct this child's wreath, fill the whole surface, including both inner and outer edges, with small bunches of prepared baby's breath attached to small wooden picks. Then attach the baby blocks on a proportionately smaller wire ring. Hot-glue the blocks with three lengths of florist's picks and, when dry, insert them into the foam base at angles to the surface of the wreath. The little trucks, boats, and cars could be exchanged for little dolls or animals. Add a grosgrain ribbon to the top of the composition and you have a great wreath to hang in a child's or grandchild's room.

99

Traditionally, the Christmas season is the time when the wreath takes a prominent stand. Evergreens abound and are used for their availability as well as their delightful aroma. Great red ribbons flow from the top of lush green wreaths, and pinecones nestle in the boughs. It is always a pleasure to take drives through neighborhoods to see the variations on this standard.

The hunting horn placed within this evergreen wreath repeats the circular form of the wreath. Apples, wired and tucked into clusters of blue cedar berries, combine with ornamental pineapples to evoke the traditional symbol of hospitality and welcome. Gold-sprayed magnolia leaves and pinecones extend the holiday festiveness.

This wreath could stand proudly as an outside decoration, or could be a perfect wreath for the den or library. Light the candles, pour some eggnog, and sit back and enjoy the holiday season.

*N*ot all holiday wreaths need an evergreen foundation to reflect the spirit of the season. A white-painted and glittered grapevine wreath becomes the base for a collection of individual tuzzy-muzzies. Each little tuzzy-muzzy or nosegay is intended to be given as a gift after a party, as the guests are departing. Sprigs of herbs, a cinnamon stick, and dried flowers are first wired together with florist's wire, then covered with gold metallic ribbon, and finally collared with gold doilies. Gold balls and long stems of painted pods add to the overall design.

You can make the tuzzy-muzzies with fresh flowers, as is the tradition, but dried flowers and herbs allow more time to prepare the lovely take-home keepsakes. Wrap some of your gifts to match the colors chosen for your tuzzy-muzzies and decorate each package with a gold doily. Finally, insert the finished tuzzy-muzzies in the hollow open spaces of the vine wreath, making sure that they are secure enough to hold but can still be removed without too much trouble or awkwardness.

Another holiday celebration is this gold-dipped vine wreath filled with pods, cut palmetto, and sea-grape leaves also dipped in bright metallic gold. These festive materials are available through your local florist. Their brilliance simply sings out the joy of the holiday season. Preserved green magnolia leaves and glittered baby's breath combine with great red satin ribbons to finish off the composition.

*U*sing the most contemporary of materials, this opalescent white sparkle wreath captures the frosty, wintry feeling of the holiday season. Small packages wrapped in opalescent papers and stars, and branches treated with glitter and festive silver ribbon unite to form a full composition that brightens up a seasonal mantle or front door. Glittered white baby's breath, strands of opalescent beads, and small opalescent leaves add to the rich, sparkling texture. Most of the elements were simply glued into place with a hot-glue gun, while a few ornaments needed to be wired. The process is one of building up layers of textures and creating a density that becomes an allover volume of unified richness.

This mantle ledge holds four wire-ring wreaths, each treated individually. The popcorn wreath was first covered with paper ribbon, wrapping the wire frame tightly. The big paper bow on the top was made by unrolling the coil of paper and securing it in place with a piece of wire. Popcorn was strung in garlands, wrapped around the twisted paper, and then secured under the paper bow.

On another wire frame, this one made with a top hooklike clasp, sections of dried pineapple slices were strung. The wreath was rehooked and a thin green ribbon was tied on top covering the mechanics.

The apple heart is made just like the dried pineapple wreath. I straightened out the one side of the hooklike clasp with a pair of pliers and skewered the apples, pushing them to the other end of the frame. When the frame was full, I returned the hook to the clasp, locked the latch together with the other hook, and concealed the mechanics with a ribbon.

The cranberry wreath is again on a wire frame. First cover the frame with small lengths of silver king, tying them onto the frame with lengths of florist wire. String the cranberries and twist the strands around the wreath to a desired fullness. Tie off the ends and place a small, thin ribbon bow on the side of the wreath just for fun. These little wreaths make wonderful holiday gifts. They are rather simple to construct, and it is something the whole family would enjoy doing together. Add them to your Christmas packages with a fresh sprig of holly or evergreen.

This brightly painted little village nestled under a great tree is made from pre-cut wooden shapes, all purchased through craft stores. The tree was cut by hand to conform to the scale of the wreath. All the small animals on the tree were pre-cut and sold in a group. All the stars, the houses, and the great tree were hot-glued to six-inch florist's picks and inserted in the evergreen frame. Thirty-six candy canes were left in their wrappers, wired onto florist's picks, and placed around the wreath. Lots of bright bleached baby's breath was used to simulate the snow and wonderland nature of the scene. In making a wreath using wooden elements, remember to paint the pieces with water-base acrylic paint. It can stand up to the harsh winter weather if the wreath is hung outdoors.

A traditional evergreen wreath rings in holiday cheer with a cascade of brass bells emanating from a cluster of gold balls and larger brass bells. The gold metallic ribbon and strand of beads that wrap around the wreath add to the texture of this holiday creation. It is an easy way to dress up a purchased evergreen wreath and at the same time create your own unique holiday statement. Substitute the bells with sprayed pinecones or Christmas-tree balls and you can achieve a similar look without the expense of the brass bells. It is not important that you have the same materials as illustrated in this book. Many substitutions work equally well.

his crab-apple-and-popcorn heart was executed on a wire frame that was first covered with boxwood—huckleberry or any seasonal green would also work. Once the heart was wound with waxed twine the apples were put into place. First they were secured to florist's picks, then inserted into the greens. The tension of the wrapped greens along the wire frame is sufficient to hold the apples and picks. A garland of popcorn was wound around the heart and secured at the top of the heart. To hide the construction, as well as to enrich the festiveness of this welcoming heart, a red satin ribbon was tied to a bow with flowing ends. Another version of this heart could include small oranges, a lemon, a lime, or apples. If fruit isn't at hand, glue some nuts to florist's picks and use them.

114

This twig-and-evergreen heart actually consists of two different wire heart frames. The larger one holds the evergreens and was constructed by placing small amounts of fresh evergreen on the wire frame and winding them securely with waxed twine. The twig heart, with small holiday balls and red berries, was constructed in the same manner, but care was taken to add the balls and berries as the winding process developed. Both sides of the twig heart began at the lower point of the heart frame and worked up to the center. There, a bow of two green ribbons and a cluster of multicolored balls cover the construction.

This traditional fresh green wreath with dried strawflowers and gold-sprayed dried grape clusters is made on a Styrofoam ring. The greens were wound with waxed twine. The strawflowers were inserted right into the Styrofoam, which holds each flower in place. A gilded strand of grapevine moves within the composition and carries out the feeling of freshness and country. Pinecones nest among the evergreen boughs, adding their own traditional presence.

116

*T*his wreath made of large pieces of cinnamon glued onto a Styrofoam ring is an aromatic pleasure to have inside. Clusters of pomander, clove-filled oranges, a lime, and a lemon, each tied with gold cord, are gifts that can be removed, leaving a permanent wreath of cinnamon sticks, pinecones, and silver king. The initial process takes some time and is best done with either designer tacky glue or a hot-glue gun.

117

Finding an abundance of shells and pinecones, and drying some artichokes became the inspiration for this rather architecturally grand holiday wreath. Using a straw ring for the foundation, I hot-glued each shell and pinecone to four-inch florist's picks. The artichokes and a few selected shells and pinecones were lightly sprayed gold and attached with florist's picks. A handsome contrast between deep rich browns and shades of orange set off the white sand dollars and scallop shells. A gold-and-white cording stiffened with wire forms an articulated bow with streamer which floats down among the shells.

119

*S*traw rings work very well as simple chandeliers for the holidays. Take a ring, measure the distance from the ceiling to where you wish it to hang, and cut to length three pieces of sturdy grosgrain ribbon—red always comes to mind, but any color would do. Allow enough ribbon to go around the straw ring and tie a secure knot. When you have tied three knots, and the balance of the wreath has been adjusted, you may have to move the ribbon a little to the left or right until the wreath floats parallel over the table. Then tie the three ribbon lengths together at the top and hang over a hook from the ceiling. Visit your local florist and purchase four plastic candleholders that have two long prongs coming from the base. Insert the prongs through the straw wreath. If they go all the way through, snip the ends off with a heavy-duty pair of wire cutters or garden shears. Make three separate bows from your ribbon and attach them at the junctions of each vertical ribbon support around the ring. Add any available fresh greens, and clusters of candy canes. Here I have also added some red berries. It is very important to remember that your greens must never be near the candles or they could burn.

Another possibility is to hang cookies or children's drawings with the candy canes. Cut out favorite Christmas-card pictures from past years and add them. It is really up to you to find what's just right for your table.

his peppermint-candy wreath is a great festive centerpiece and is also edible. Alternating stripes of wrapped peppermint candies and boxwood circle the Styrofoam wreath form. A very easy way to make this centerpiece is to take three or four candies in their wrappers and wire them together with a two-inch florist's pick. The picks come with a wire attached. This process fills the spaces quickly, keeps the candy safe and clean in their wrappers, and doesn't require much effort or time. The boxwood is cut into short lengths and inserted directly into the Styrofoam. Add some metallic or plaid ribbon bows and fill the center with tall taper candles in brass candlesticks, or circle the centerpiece with tiny votive candles in glass containers. Everyone will find this the sweetest of wreaths.

A real kitchen wreath for the holidays is made out of a loaf of Italian braided bread that has dried and become hard. To preserve it you should coat the whole loaf, top and bottom, with a clear acrylic spray. Add greens, peppermint-candy rings, and small wooden ornaments and balls. Simply insert each element directly into the bread. A hot-glue gun will insure that they stay right where you desire. It is essential to wire the candy rings to a florist's pick. This is an easy wreath to make and would be a charming gift to give at the holiday time.

You can always speed up the drying time by placing your loaf of bread in the oven. Set the temperature on low and leave the bread in until it feels totally hard and dry. Remember to give it a protective coating before decorating it.

123

CHAPTER SIX

Unusual Uses
for Wreaths

The uses of wreaths and vines are as endless as your imagination. Aside from being beautiful decorative pieces, wreaths can be successfully incorporated into a wrapping or a presentation of a gift. The art of wrapping up a special jar of garden-grown tomatoes can be made even more special with a twist of grapevine. It is not difficult to do; just remember to lock each end of the vine into the body of the wreath. Wrap a gold-sprayed vine wreath around gifts from the kitchen and add fancy paper, or leave the vines natural and add a bit of your favorite fabric. Either way the recipient will be overjoyed by not only your gift but also your special way of presenting it.

A basket makes a perfect foundation for grapevines, because each vine can easily pass between the woven components of the basket structure. Here a vine covers the lower portion of a basket filled with moss and sprouting a beautiful bouquet of pears.

126

ou can easily "countrify" your kitchen or bathroom by wrapping a vine wreath around an apothecary's jar or a cookie jar. Fill one with soap for the guest bathroom or ornament one with strawflowers for the kitchen. During the holidays, make small wreaths from evergreens and place them around decanters. With a little imagination and creativity, your skills at wreathmaking will be put to good use all year long.

Every parent is proud of their child, and every grandparent or favorite aunt or uncle would enjoy a little wreath filled with photographs. Here the standard school photograph becomes the collection, but any photograph would do. Add a few flowers and send it off to warm the hearts of relatives far away. Again, take advantage of the variety of ready-made wreaths, as their colors and materials will often inspire an idea or remind you of someone who would greatly appreciate receiving one.

*I*t seems there are always a few flowers left over when you make a big wreath, a few extra pinecones and so on. The best way to use them up is to make a number of small wreaths using any type of foundation. Make them and save them and then use one as an ornament for a special gift. The yellow package has a pre-made cinnamon heart on it with a raffia bow. A few extra strawflowers grace the bow and bring a little color. The hearts come in three sizes and you will find a number of decorative uses for them. The mauve wreath is also pre-made and comes painted. It has been decorated with mauve baby's breath and small flowers from a larger hydrangea blossom. The ribbon is a rich, deep burgundy, and the whole package has a subtle blending of similar colors. The bright little wreath is made on a small straw base and is filled with a potpourri of colored strawflowers, some very tiny pinecones, and a few sprigs of baby's breath. A bow using cornhusks has been made for the wreath.

A Styrofoam base was covered with designer tacky glue and loose potpourri was pressed around the wreath form. This sweet, fragrant wreath has a few roses glued to the top and is anchored to the aqua gift box by an apple-green satin ribbon.

The last gift is wrapped with brown paper and tied together with a length of fresh grapevine. This piece of vine retains clusters of dried grapes. Grapevines make wonderful package wraps, but it is important to securely lock both ends of the vine into the package.

reaths as centerpieces can be very beautiful. This bright zinnia wreath has as its base a ring of oasis. Oasis is a material that when immersed in water retains the water for some time, keeping fresh flowers alive for many days.

In this example I took an oasis, wet it, and placed it on a large copper tray. With garden-picked flowers and sprigs of mint, rosemary, and sage, I've made a quick summer wreath for the table. I find using fresh flowers throughout the growing season to be one very simple and easy way to decorate a table. Oasis rings come in a number of sizes and are available at your florist's.

Moss and spring flowers offer endless possibilities for creative seasonal wreaths. Pansies, dusty miller, and freesia pop up through a rich covering of moss, celebrating the awakening of spring.

This wreath was made entirely with fresh flowers placed in water tubes. The tubes were then attached to florist's picks and inserted into a moss-covered straw base.

When autumn rolls around and the fresh flowers become increasingly hard to find, it's good to go back to dried materials and the handy glue gun. This centerpiece was constructed from a piece of plywood.

Simply cut a circle and remove the center, keeping an equal proportion for the ring. Drill four holes to fit standard candles. Hot-glue a variety of flowers, seed pods, and small pinecones to the plywood in a full, richly textured pattern of colors and forms. Because of its combination of hominess and beauty, this wreath would look equally good on either a formal table or a country-kitchen pine.

Something a bit more casual but just as functional is this Italian-bread centerpiece. Protect the bread against moisture by using acrylic spray. Make sure to really coat it well to prevent the bread from changing after you apply your decorations.

Ornament the ring of bread with small clusters of strawflowers, eucalyptus, a few pieces of lichen and moss, and a couple hydrangeas, and finish it off with a few strategically placed candles.

These three candle rings are simply three examples of an endless variety of solutions for the base of a candle. Two bases were cut from plywood and one is a wire ring. In making the wire ring I used the winding method to apply baby's breath and pinecones with white painted ends. It is an easy process and quickly makes a festive base.

The two wooden bases have a ribbon of woven fiber glued to the outer edge of the ring, and are finished off with a flat bow. Here, again, I used my trusty hot-glue gun to attach the ribbon to the wooden ring. The top of the ring surface is covered with sheet moss, with individual miniature pods glued into random clusters. Finally, I added tiny pinecones into the deep monochrome palette of the pods and moss. These little wreaths are small, easy to make, and a good way to use up some left-over materials. However, if the candle is burning it should never be left unattended.

The wreath in the foreground is on a wooden ring that is totally covered with moss. In this case, the moss covers the whole outer edge of the ring, eliminating the need for a ribbon. Strawflowers, bits of eucalyptus, and a few pieces of dried sage mix to form a rich, full wreath.

When the summer birds leave their homes, and the winter winds chill the air, it is time to make a few very special wreaths just for the birds. This small grapevine wreath that has been tied to the top of a painted birdhouse is filled with clusters of pinecones stuffed with peanut butter and a variety of seeds. I enjoy watching the birds eat from small wreaths placed around the yard. You can easily hang them from tree limbs and from your porch. It is possible, of course, to make larger feeding wreaths using combinations of standard winter feeding materials. Experiment and enjoy the challenge. I often include orange slices, grapes, popcorn, and cranberries, as well as oats and other summer grasses. The squirrels will also thank you for providing them with tasty treats.

139

*T*his book has provided you with a great number of ideas as well as instructions for making your own wreaths. The step-by-step procedures will help, as will the tips in finding or preserving flowers and pods. It is always recommended that you frequent your local florist, favorite craft shop, or garden center and look for the familiar and unfamiliar materials that they carry. Don't be afraid to ask questions or to experiment with what you are working with. The more control you develop the richer your experiences will become, and the more pleasure you will derive from making wreaths. I cannot stress enough that you should approach wreathmaking with an attitude that indeed you can do it and that you can freely interpret the way in which your wreath develops. Be flexible, as that will bring you more rewarding pleasure and give you the best creative results. Mostly, I wish you the courage to try and satisfaction in having done so.

Sources

Hallmark Cards
25th and McGee
Kansas City, Mo. 64108

Ask for the KNUD NIELSEN label when buying dried materials: twigs, pods, and natural design accessories.

Aleene's Thick Designer Tacky Glue
Aleene's Artist Inc.
Box 407
Solvang, California 93463
(805) 688-7339

Thermogrip® brand hot melt glue gun
Thermogrip® brand glue sticks
c/o Emhart Home Products Division
P.O. Box 13716
Reading, Pa. 19612
(800) 537-5000

Thumbprint Antiques
Old Tongore Road
Stone Ridge, N.Y.
(914) 687-9318